THE LIFE AND WISDOM OF
FRANCIS
XAVIER

THE LIFE AND WISDOM OF

FRANCIS XAVIER

Written and Compiled by

LAVINIA BYRNE

Hodder & Stoughton

LONDON SYDNEY AUCKLAND

British Library Cataloguing in Publication Data:
A record for this book is available from the British Library.

ISBN 0 340 70957 8

Typeset in Monotype Columbus by
Strathmore Publishing Services, London N7.

Printed and bound in Great Britain by
Mackays of Chatham PLC, Chatham, Kent.

Hodder and Stoughton Ltd,
A division of Hodder Headline PLC,
338 Euston Road, London NW1 3BH

CONTENTS

———————◆———————

CONTENTS

INTRODUCTION

Who are the saints and why should we bother to know about their lives? We are inclined to think of them as heroic people who did extraordinary things, or as people who suffered a great deal and were somehow specially gifted or good. What we then forget is that, in general, saints are people like us. They struggled to know themselves better, to be more kind and loving, more self-accepting, less neurotic. They did not always succeed. They thought their attempts to live with integrity would make them closer to other people and to God. Often what they then discovered was that other people became harder to love and that God simply disappeared.

Yet they kept up the struggle. They believed that they were given one chance, that they had to live with a certain generosity, because this life is a preparation for the full glory of the next life. They then learnt that we are given many chances because all is grace, and the Christian life is a life of grace. So their schemes and plans for being holy were dismantled. All that was asked of them was a readiness to accept the gifts of God, including the final gift of heaven.

Saints come from every walk of life. They are men and women who share our concerns about money, power, politics, peace, energy, food, war, death, sex, love, privacy, the inner life, the outer life, harmony, balance. What makes them distinctive is that they looked beyond themselves to know how best to live and they discovered that God shared their concerns. If we read about them nowadays, we do so out of more than simple curiosity. Their lives are worth reading because we can learn from them. We look for more than a good example, though. The saints seem to know more than we do; they have access to a deeper level of wisdom than our own. They are gurus for our times. So when we read about them, we are quite right to seek an insight into the mind of God, who calls and inspires us all to the heroism of holiness, however we ourselves happen to live. Holiness is for all, not just the few; for a holy life is no more than a life lived in the presence of God.

In our materialistic and agnostic age, do the saints still matter? Have they any wisdom for us, or are they simply a pious irrelevance? Are their lives mere legends, or do they have some significance beyond the bare bones of what history tells us about them?

Over the past twenty years there has been a revival of interest in Christian spirituality. Many of us go on retreat or enjoy 'quiet days'; many of us are able to take part in Church life in ways which were unimaginable previously; many of us are able to question our faith and belief systems because we are prepared to see how they fit in with the rest of our lives. An important part of this spiritual revival has been the experience of Ignatian spirituality, a way of 'seeking and finding God in all things' – a God who is present in all things, absent from none.

Francis Xavier, the apostle of the Indies, was one of Ignatius' first friends and followers. His life story is about a remarkable commitment to mission, to journeys of adventure and exploration which took him to the furthest parts of the known world. His is a fascinating life, a life charged with the love of Christ and the certainty that 'the journey is our home'. In examining the life of Xavier, we gain an insight into the heart and mindset of Ignatius, and also into our own.

In his *Life of John Dryden*, Sir Walter Scott wrote,

> There are few who can read, without a sentiment of admiration, the heroic devotion with which from the highest principles of duty, Xavier exposes himself to hardship, to danger, to death itself, that he may win souls to the Christian faith. The most rigid Protestant, and the most indifferent philosopher, cannot deny to him the courage and patience of a martyr, with the good sense, resolution, ready wit, and address, of the best negotiator that ever went upon a temporal embassy.

A Presbyterian biographer of Xavier subtitled her book 'Explorer, Evangelist and Mystic'. Who was Francis Xavier and how can his universal appeal be explained?

PART ONE

The Story of His Early Years: Gentleman, *hidalgo* and nobleman

Xavier the magnanimous, the holy and the gay;
the canonised saint, not of Rome only, but of
universal Christendom

— *The Edinburgh Review, 1842*

Xavier the magnanimous student

We, the Emperor, Queen and King, by this present definitive sentence pronounce and declare Don Francisco de Jassu y Xavier to be of ancient lineage, and as such empower him and his sons and descendants in direct line to use and enjoy all the prerogatives, exemptions, honours, offices, liberties, privileges, landed property and duelling rights which appertain to gentlemen, *hidalgos* and noblemen in our Kingdom of Navarre and everywhere else.

This is an adventure story, a romance. Its central

character is Francis Xavier, one-time gentleman, *hidalgo* and nobleman, now a saint – the 'apostle of the Indies'. When Xavier received his certificate of nobility from Emperor Charles V, he was twenty-nine years old. The date was 1535. He was a student in Paris and poised to leave the University after ten years of study there. With six friends he was about to set off on a journey to fulfil a vow they had made on 15 August of the previous year. They were going to go to Jerusalem, or so they thought. In the event they spent a year in Venice, hoping for a boat and a passage to Palestine, praying to know God's purpose and intentions for them, before making their way to Rome and an uncertain future.

They had been friends for quite a while. Francis Xavier, Peter Favre, Alfonso Salmeron, Simon Rodriguez, Diego Lainez and Nicolas Bobadilla formed a disparate group, but they had one thing in common: they were followers of a man called Ignatius Loyola. We know Ignatius as the founder of the Society of Jesus. Francis Xavier was one of his earliest companions, a founding Jesuit. As the Society's first great missionary, he was to embody some of its most telling ideals and qualities. For his was a life of obedience, and in the name of obedience to God he would travel thousands of miles to the remotest countries of the East, venturing to places no European had ever visited before.

Early years

When Xavier first met Ignatius, he did not take to him. They came from the same part of the world, the Basque country, to the north of Spain. They both had a similar background as 'gentlemen, *hidalgos* and noblemen', but Ignatius walked with a limp and did not cut much of a dash when they met in 1529. He had gained his limp as a result of an injury sustained during the battle of Pamplona – a skirmish in one of the wars which Francis I of France and Charles V of Spain waged on each other. The irony is that Xavier's two brothers had been at the same battle – on the French side. Historians have wondered if one of them fired the offending shot: the shot which laid Ignatius low and caused him to spend many hours alone on his sickbed at Loyola, wrestling with the demands of the gospel, seeking God's will at a time of great personal need, developing the core insights about discernment which would inspire the rest of his life.

Xavier's initial reaction to Ignatius is understandable. If he was a Spanish nobleman, why had he arrived in Paris with all his books strapped to the back of a donkey? At thirty-eight, was he not too old to be studying, as well as suspiciously religious? Besides, Xavier had a friend already and shared his digs with him at the College of Sante-Barbe on what is nowadays the Boulevard St Michel. Peter Favre was keener on his work that Xavier and more disciplined in keeping to the rigorous programme which the students had to follow. An account of it is given by another of them, one Henri de Mesmes:

> We were up at 4 a.m. and, having said our prayers, trailed an hour later to the hall of studies, with our big books under our arms and our inkpots and candlesticks in our hands. There was no break in the lessons until 10 o'clock, when we were given something to eat. After

dinner we read by way of recreation Sophocles, Aristophanes or Eurypides, and sometimes Demosthenes, Cicero, Vergil and Horace. At 1 o'clock, we began private study. We had supper at 6 o'clock and then read more Greek or Latin.

Xavier's petition to the Emperor to have his nobility recognised dates from this time. A licence to be recognised, a licence to duel and have fun, must have seemed an extremely attractive alternative to the endless Greek and Latin. His home was not the grandest of places, but Xavier's lawyer father and rather more nobly bred mother had managed to provide him with a good enough, and deeply religious, education, as well as the qualifications for nobility. Whereas his brothers went to war and married well, Francis Xavier took a more scholarly route. His future would be secured with a degree from Paris. What he intended to do with it is unclear, though the Church offered one possibility.

Then he met Ignatius and, despite early misgivings, gradually fell under his spell. What was this spell and how did it change Xavier's life?

There was the personal charisma, of course. Ignatius was a man of fire. He had the capacity to make a powerful impact on other people because he was himself set alight by a vision of great glory and fascination. He wanted to preach the gospel in a new way; he wanted people to experience the power of God's love. He was a man with a story and he wanted other people to get to know their own story, so that through its complexities they should see God at work. God, to Ignatius' mind, was present in the events of human life. To discover God at work, all that was needed was a discerning heart.

Ignatius offered his young followers more than the fire of his own personality; he offered them an experience. It was contained in a series of exercises which he had developed while struggling to understand his own story. Nowadays they are known as *The Spiritual Exercises of Saint Ignatius*. They transformed the life of Francis Xavier; they continue to transform lives today.

The Spiritual Exercises

Francis Xavier was twenty-eight years old when

he made the Exercises in September 1534. Ignatius later said of him that he was the hardest of his companions to form. His secretary, Polanco, noted, 'I have heard our great modeller of men, Ignatius, say that Francis Xavier was, at first, the stiffest clay he had ever handled.' When Xavier made the Spiritual Exercises, what was he letting himself in for? A retreat, in the first instance. That is to say, he withdrew for a month of prayer and reflection. In silence he presented himself to God. In silence he underwent the process of transformation which Ignatius had learnt on his sickbed in the castle at Loyola and subsequently in a cave at Manresa, near Monserrat. Just as Ignatius had struggled to understand the leanings of his own heart, now Xavier would do the same thing.

At Loyola, Ignatius had read the lives of Saint Francis of Assisi and of Saint Dominic. There had been no adventure stories or romances available to while away the long hours he spent recovering from his shattered leg (surgeons had to re-break it in an attempt to straighten it further). Instead he had tried Ludovic of Saxony's

Life of Christ. He began to notice what he felt as he read. He saw that the delight he experienced when he read romances or storybooks somehow failed to last. The saints' lives, however, stayed with him. He underlined the words of Jesus in the gospel stories and noted what attracted him. Above all, he daydreamed, letting his imagination roam far and wide. He discovered that it was his friend, an ally to be trusted in the quest for God and for the divine will.

In the cave at Manresa, these experiences were deepened. He practised fasting; he let his hair grow long; he experimented with asceticism. A strange, serpent-like being began to haunt him, with glowing eyes on its body. He saw an image of the Trinity – like three keys on a keyboard playing one harmonious melody; he saw God creating light at the start of creation; he walked by a deep river and was consoled by a sense of profound enlightenment. Later he would write of himself: 'And this left him with the understanding enlightened in so great a way that it seemed to him as if he were a different person, and he had another mind, different from that which he had before.' He gave up the fasting and cut his hair and nails. He understood that the serpent-like creature was a harmful illusion. He had his eyes fixed on God. This was the experience he now most wanted to share with other people. His Spiritual Exercises were no more – and no less – than a scheme to help them experience the total transformation to which he had submitted himself. They were the most precious gift he could give to Xavier, or to any of his first companions.

The Exercises were grouped in such a way that they could be followed over a four-week period, with the opportunity for a break at the end of each of the four 'weeks'. During the first of these, Xavier was asked to pray with stories taken from the Scriptures: those of the fall of Adam and Eve. The invitation was to an experience of grace, and most especially the grace of forgiveness. If Ignatius asked him to think about sin and human evil, this was because he knew that only a sinner can turn to God for forgiveness. The first week's exercises recall us to our truest destiny. We are the beloved sons and daughters of God. We can turn to God with a great shout of joy, a cry of recognition.

The exercises of the second week remind us that Ignatius was a soldier as well as a layman when he first began to develop the ideas, which is one of the reasons why they are such a powerful tool for conversion. Xavier was asked to imagine an earthly king, someone to whom he could offer his allegiance, an emperor perhaps, certainly as fine a leader as the one to whom he had written seeking recognition as a gentleman, *hidalgo* and nobleman. Then he was to think of the person of Christ and to see that all the qualities he most admired in an earthly king were even more abundantly and reliably present in his heavenly king. What would his reaction be? Ignatius anticipates generosity, a spirit of service, the desire to sacrifice all for so great a Lord.

Then he changes the canvas completely. The stage shifts to a contemplation of the three persons of the Blessed Trinity. They are depicted on some heavenly balcony, looking at the earth from afar, concerned about the fate of humanity and resolved to do something about it. The angel

Gabriel is sent to a girl called Mary in a city called Nazareth. From this moment on, Xavier's fate was sealed. He was caught up into an enthralling dynamic: the salvation of the world is only possible when someone is sent – an angel holds the destiny of the world in its wings. Heaven stands still, earth is silent. And in the ensuing dialogue, Mary accepts the gift of the Christ child into the very fabric of her body. Mission – the sending of the Word into the world – is all. The missionary most truly fulfils God's purpose.

With the incarnation of God's son, the story of Adam and Eve is reversed. Salvation becomes possible. The Word is spoken and can now be proclaimed. Xavier would have spent the rest of the second week of the Exercises reflecting on the ways in which God embraces humanity – first as a baby on the straw, then as a growing child, and finally as the fisher of men who called disciples and apostles to his service, sending them in turn, two by two, to cast out devils and proclaim the word: 'The kingdom of God is near, repent and believe.'

Jesus' own proclamation of the word brought him to the place of judgment and suffering: to the cross. In the third week of the Exercises, Ignatius has his retreatant follow him there, for mission is about realism as well. Those who are sent on the same flight path as the angel Gabriel are driven inexorably to the cross. Here we are most truly judged and most truly redeemed. We watch and pray with the women who stood their ground at the feet of the dying Jesus; we wait with his mother; we become the beloved disciples; we hear his seven last words. We stand by helplessly as he says, 'I thirst'; we die with him.

Only in this way can we rise with him. And this is precisely what the fourth week of the Exercises anticipates. When Francis Xavier himself died, in the harbour of Sancian at the age of forty-six, did he remember this moment? For Ignatius has his retreatant contemplate the wholeness of all things, a dispensation of grace where all is gift and the God who dwells in all creatures, in the elements, plants and animals as well as in human beings, labours on our behalf. In response to the generosity of God, the young

Francis Xavier would have prayed, 'Take, Lord, and receive all my liberty, my memory, my understanding and my entire will, all that I have and possess. You gave it all to me; to you Lord I give it all back. All is yours, dispose of it entirely according to your will. Give me the grace to love you, for that is enough for me.'

The years of preparation

Before God took up the offer Xavier had made during his retreat, there was further spadework to be done. Not only was he being formed, his companions were, too. The Society of Jesus began in obscurity, however gifted the young men who first heard God's call. Cervantes would later write, 'These first Jesuits were mirrors reflecting holiness, pure doctrine, a singular prudence and a profound humility.' They earned such a reputation at some cost.

Their year in Venice was spent praying and taking care of the sick and needy. Simon Rodriguez described a typical day in the hospital where they worked:

We made the beds, swept the floors, emptied and scoured utensils, cleaned up the wards generally, carried the bodies of the dead reverently to the graves we had dug for them, and day and night attended hand and foot on the sick, with so much satisfaction and joy that we astonished those living at the hospital and even attracted the attention of eminent persons in the city, who came to stare at our activities as at something wonderful.

The gifted, scholarly young noblemen could not fail to make an impact by the quality of their care for the poor and needy, as well as by the fervour of their devotional life.

After a journey to Rome to establish a relationship between the Pope and the nascent Society of Jesus, Xavier and his friends returned to Venice. He was ordained priest there. Vincenzo Nigusanti, the Bishop of Arbe, ordained all of the first companions except Salmeron, who was too young, on the Feast of St John the Baptist, 24 June 1537. They went on working in Venice, still concerned to travel on to

Jerusalem to visit the Holy Land. When the date which they had set themselves as a deadline came and went, they abandoned their project and set off back to Rome to offer their services to Pope Paul III. Xavier stopped off in Bologna on the way. A priest there recorded his impressions of the Spaniard:

> He was a man slow to speak, but whose words when he did speak went straight to people's hearts. At Mass, particularly if it was a Mass of the Passion of Christ, he wept abundant tears. One Friday, while saying Mass in the church of Saint Lucia, he was so wrapt out of himself for more than an hour at the Memento, though the server tried hard to rouse him by tugging at his vestments. After Mass he would spend the entire day hearing confession, visiting the sick in the hospitals and prisoners in the gaols, serving the poor, preaching in the piazza, and teaching children or other uninstructed persons Christian doctrine. Though very ill all the while, he never omitted his early morning prayer, or his Mass, or any of his daily avocations.

Once in Rome, the brethren began to separate again. Theirs was not to be a gathered community, with a way of life built around the monastic hours or regular prayer said in common. They were to be a dispersed or a missionary community. The Pope himself had commented to them, 'Why are you so anxious to go to Jerusalem? Is not Italy a good and true Jerusalem if you desire to bear fruit in the Church of God?' So at first they worked within Italy. Xavier remained in Rome, acting as secretary to Ignatius while he drew up a founding document for the new society. Paul III approved this document verbally on 3 September 1539 and the following September it was confirmed with the papal bull *Regimini militantis ecclesiae*. The Society of Jesus was born.

By the spring of 1540, four of Ignatius' companions had already been commissioned for overseas service: two for Ireland and two for India. The two due to go to India were Rodriguez and Bobadilla. Then, just before he was to set off for Lisbon to catch a ship for India, Bobadilla fell ill. Ignatius sent for Xavier and told him that he was to go to India in Bobadilla's stead.

So Xavier set off for the ship at Lisbon, and began the long journey which would take him to India, Japan and on to China. Did he know that he was saying a final farewell to Ignatius and to the other companions with whom he had shared so much? The years of preparation were over. Now he would begin his true work.

Lisbon

Xavier arrived in Lisbon at the end of June 1540. Simon Rodriguez was already there, but he too had been struck down with sickness. The two men would have to wait before they could travel. Meanwhile, the King and Queen commanded the two Jesuits to visit them and undertook to provide them with food during their stay. Lisbon was an extraordinarily cosmopolitan city, teeming with Indians and Africans, merchants and slaves. It was a prosperous city, with trade routes that led east and west. The Church was undergoing a tempestuous time, as the Inquisition was in full flood and heretics were regularly burnt at the stake there. Xavier wrote to Ignatius:

The Infante Dom Henrique, brother of the King and chief Inquisitor of the Kingdom, has exhorted us on numerous occasions to look after the prisoners of the Inquisition. We visit them every day and do our best to help them to recognise that it is the mercy of God which has put them where they are. On each visit, we preach to them collectively and give them meditations from the first 'week' of the *Spiritual Exercises*, from which they have derived no small profit. Several of them have told us that God our Lord has done them a great favour by thus bringing them to a knowledge of many things necessary for the salvation of their souls.

Many of these prisoners of the Inquisition were casualties of campaigns by Spain and Portugal to expel all Moors and Jews from their midst. People of mixed race were treated as religious heretics. What was the Church to do with the infidel? Was persecution the only answer? Xavier wrote to Ignatius, raising some of his anxieties with him. These were questions which would become much more important as he worked in

the Far East, but already here in Portugal they
began to prey on his consciousness.

> By the love and service of God our Lord we
> pray you to write next March when the ships
> leave Portugal for India. Tell us what, in your
> opinion, ought to be our method with the
> unbelievers. Although experience will teach us
> partly how we ought to go about it, yet for the
> rest we hope in God our Lord that it will please
> His Divine Majesty to make us to know
> through you the best way in which to serve
> Him. He has done so until now, but we are
> afraid of what often happens, and has been the
> fate of so many. By carelessness, or by not being
> willing to ask others and take advice from them,
> they are denied many things by God. What
> counsels have you? What means shall we use for
> the better service of God our Lord? We do wish
> to have the will of Christ our Lord made clear
> to us through you. Again we ask you – have us
> in your prayers beyond the new dealing with
> heathen, and our ignorance, ask for much more
> favour that usual.

While waiting for an answer, as well as for the fleet of ships to be prepared, Xavier and Rodriguez ran two different apostolates, or missions, in tandem during the time they spent in Lisbon. On the one hand they administered the sacraments, spending hours hearing the confessions of the knights and courtiers who were on permanent service to the King and Queen. On the other they developed their own specialist ministry, discovering that the Spiritual Exercises of Ignatius had other applications which could serve their purposes. The experience of the Exercises gave people a new sense of self and renewed them at the deepest core of their being. So successful was their ministry that the King became increasingly reluctant to see them go. In the end it was decided that Rodriguez should remain in Portugal. Xavier, meanwhile, acquired two new companions, Paul of Camerino and Francis Mansilhas.

They had six months to wait before a fleet would be ready. Xavier continued to reflect on the missionary enterprise that faced him. As he wrote to Ignatius:

From India, with the first ships that leave, we shall write fully, and tell you all about everything. The King said to me when I took my leave that I was to write very fully for the love of our Lord about the opportunity there is there for the conversion of those poor souls. He takes their misery hard, and was very anxious that their Creator and Redeemer might not be perpetually shamed by the creatures made in His image and likeness, and bought with such a price.

Then he took his leave with these words:

There is nothing else to tell you but when we are to embark. In concluding, we pray Christ our Lord to give us the grace to see each other, and to bring us together in the other life bodily. For in this life I do not know if we shall see each other again, both because of the great distance from Rome to India, and because of the great harvest, which is there without going to seek it elsewhere. And let the first of us that goes to the other life, and does not find his brother whom he loves in the

Lord, pray Christ our Lord to join us all there
in His glory.

Eventually the great day came and on 7 April
1541, his own birthday, Xavier set sail for Goa in
India. He was thirty-five years old. He went
confident that he was called to the service of his
Creator and Redeemer, that the people to whom
he would minister were his fellow human beings,
made by the same God who had made him, and
that Christ's blood had been shed for them as it
had for him. The gentleman, *hidalgo* and nobleman had found a new identity: in India he would
become the evangelist, explorer and mystic of his
dreams.

PART TWO

The Wisdom of Francis Xavier:
'For to be good we have to be pilgrims in this life'

The sea voyage

While he was working at the hospital in Bologna, Xavier had had a dream and had cried out in his sleep about a burden he was trying to carry: 'Jesus, how crushed and fatigued I feel! Do you know what I dreamt? – that I was trying to hoist an Indian on my shoulders, and he was such a deadly weight I couldn't lift him.' On the thirteen-month passage to Goa, he began to shoulder this burden in earnest. The ship, called the *Santiago,* was meant to take eight months to reach India, but no sooner had they embarked than scurvy broke out among the thousand men on board.

Xavier and his two companions threw themselves into the task of taking care of the sick, nursing them, washing their clothes and bringing them food. Then they were becalmed for forty days off the coast of Guinea. As soon as any wind arose, the *Santiago* headed out into the open sea, taking the longest possible route around the Cape and then coming back towards Mozambique. By then they had been at sea for five months. Because so many of the sailors were sick, Dom Martim Affonso de Souza, the captain of the fleet with whom they were sailing, decided that they should winter in the Portuguese port in Mozambique.

A vivid portrait of this journey and its hazards comes from the pen of another Jesuit, an Italian named Valignano, who went to India from Lisbon in 1574.

The perils and hardships suffered on this expedition are very extensive and terrifying. The first hardship is lack of accommodation. True, the ships are large and powerful, but so packed with passengers, merchandise and provisions that there is little room left for any one to move about, and the ordinary people aboard, for whose comfort there is no arrangement whatever, must stand all day on deck in the blazing sun and sleep there somehow all night in the cold. On the other hand, the berths put at the disposal of noble or wealthy persons are so low, so narrow, so confined, that it is all a man can do to fit himself into them. The second hardship has to do with food and drink. Though his Highness the King provides daily rations of biscuit, meat, fish, water and wine sufficient to keep the passengers alive, the meat and fish are so salty, and the provision of utensils to collect the rations so inadequate, that the suffering on this account, especially among the soldiers, beggars description. The third hardship among the general run of the voyagers is due to their being poor and happy-go-lucky. They set out with insufficient clothing, the little they bring soon rots on their backs, and they suffer dreadfully in lower latitudes, both from the cold and from the stench of their rags. The fourth hardship is caused by the calms off the Guinea Coast, which may last for forty, fifty or sixty days. During that time the passengers almost sweat their souls out and suffer torments from the heat beyond the power of my pen to set forth. The fifth hardship, and the worst of any, is the lack of water. During much of the voyage, the water doled out in the daily ration is so foul and malodorous that it is impossible to bear the stench of it, and the passengers have to put a piece of cloth before their mouths to filter off the corruption. This liquid is distributed only once a day, and many fail to get their portion through having nothing in which to collect it. Others drink their entire ration at one gulp, the result being that large numbers die of thirst. The sixth hardship results from disease of every description among the passengers, who suffer a thousand miseries before dying or recovering. The King appoints a surgeon to each ship, but he and his remedies soon cease to be of any use.

When they landed in Mozambique, Xavier and his companions went to the shore hospital with the sick, of whom eighty promptly died. Xavier himself soon fell ill, but on his recovery he began to preach and teach amongst the townspeople, gathering them into church on Sunday or going out amongst them on weekdays, attracting crowds to listen to him.

When the time came to set sail again – this time in a ship called the *Coulam* – the Governor of the island asked for Xavier's two companions to remain behind to take care of the sick. Paul of Camerino and Francis Mansilhas duly stayed in Mozambique.

Xavier set off on the next leg of his journey, which took him to Melinda on the African coast. This was a Muslim city. It had seventeen mosques, but only three of these were in active use. Islam had fallen on hard times and stood in as much need of reform as the scattered Christian communities Xavier met on his journey. Socotra, an island off the Gulf of Aden, was an example of these. When the *Coulam* berthed there, he found a native Christian community. Their Muslim overlords left them in peace, but they practised a debased sort of Christianity, knowing nothing of baptism and praying in an ancient language which Xavier took to be Chaldean. He assumed the islanders had been original converts from the time of St Thomas, the apostle of Jesus who first took the gospel to India. Most likely they were actually Nestorian or Assyrian converts from the fifth century. As the sheer strangeness of the situation in which he found himself began to dawn upon him, Xavier wrote about them to Ignatius:

The people of this island are Christians in their own opinion; so they regard themselves; they boast a lot of being Christians; in their names they show it; they are a very ignorant folk; they can neither read nor write; they have no books nor writings . . . they have churches and crosses and lamps. Each place has its *caciz,* he is like a cleric among us. These *cacizes* can neither read nor write, and have neither books nor writings. They know numbers of prayers by heart. They go to church at midnight and in the morning, at the hour of vespers, and in the afternoons at the hour of compline – four times a day. They have no bells, they call the people with wooden clappers as we do in Holy Week. Even the *cacizes* do not understand the prayers, for they are not in their own language; I believe they are in Chaldean. I wrote down three or four of the prayers that they use. I was twice in this island.

They are devoted to St Thomas; they say they are come from the Christians which he made in those parts. In their prayers these *cacizes* sometimes say Aleluya, aleluya; they pronounce it almost as we do. They do not baptise, nor do they know what baptism is.

I was at vespers said by a *caciz;* he took an hour to say them, and never did anything but cense and pray. Those *cazices* are married, great fasters; when they fast they do not eat fish nor milk nor flesh – they would rather die. Although there is plenty of fish on the island, they keep themselves on dates and herbs. They fast two Lents, and one is for two months. Those who are not *cacizes* do not enter the church if they are eating meat in these Lents, nor do the women go there.

There were stranger things to come, but as they began the next leg of their journey, the travellers' thoughts turned to Vasco da Gama, the great Portuguese explorer who had opened up trade routes between the Mediterranean and the Indies over forty years earlier. Pedro Alvarez Cabral had followed close on his heels, bringing men and ships and soldiers with him to develop the trade links. Pepper, spices, jewels and cloth travelled west, while Franciscans and Dominican missionaries travelled east in the wake of the soldiers and sailors who first colonised the area. Soon every fortified trading station on the coast had its resident priest to care for the garrison. At Goa a diocese was established with its own cathedral and bishop. When Xavier landed there on 6 May 1542, he went immediately to the bishop's rather grand residence.

First steps in Goa

The bishop recommended a smart house for Xavier too. He resisted this idea, however, and chose instead to live amongst the poorest people, sleeping at night on a rush mat and working by day in the hospital and hearing confessions. In the afternoons he took himself off to the leper hospital and worked there. On Sundays he would say Mass for the lepers at the Church of Our Lady. He would walk about with a little bell, ringing it to gather a crowd of people together and then preach to them. He set the catechism of Catholic teaching to music and taught the simple tunes and words to the children. Wherever he went, he spoke to people about the love and excellence of God.

When the rainy season ended, he was to be off on the road again, going this time to Cape Comorin on the southernmost tip of India where the three oceans meet. Pearl fishermen there had been forcibly baptised by earlier Portuguese missionaries. The local people had called in the Portuguese when under threat of invasion from some Muslim antagonists. Although the priests had not spoken a word of the natives' language, they had baptised twenty thousand of them and then left them to it. The new viceroy – Xavier's former sea captain, now turned diplomat – Dom Martim de Souza became their advocate when once again they were invaded by Muslims. He sent to the Bishop of Goa and asked if Xavier could come to their aid. Towards the end of September 1542, he set off, taking two young Indian catechists and a deacon with him to act as interpreters and fellow workers. They set sail for

Cochin, intending to walk from there to a base at Tuticorin.

Bringing the gospel to the pearl fishing community
Xavier threw himself into the work he met. There were partial Christians to be instructed in the rudiments of their faith; there were unbelievers to be brought to Christ. The pearl fishing community was desperately poor; he wanted to offer them the pearl of greatest price, namely the Christian gospel. He worked ceaselessly and wrote home unsentimental, factual accounts of what he was trying to do.

> On our way here we came through some villages where the people had become Christians eight years ago. There are no Portuguese living there now, as the country is extremely sterile and very poor. As they have no one to teach them our faith, the Christians of these villages know no more of it than to say that they are Christians. They have no one to say Mass, still less to teach them the Creed, *Pater noster, Ave Maria,* or the Commandments. When I arrived

in these places I baptised all the children who were not baptised, so that I baptised a great multitude of infants *who could not distinguish between their right hand and their left*. When I came to these places the children would not let me read my office nor eat nor sleep, but made me teach them some prayers. I began to understand then that *of such is the kingdom of heaven*. As I could not refuse such a holy petition, I taught them, beginning with the confession of the Father, Son and Holy Spirit, with the Creed, *Pater noster, Ave Maria*. I recognised great gifts in them, and if there were anyone to teach them the holy faith, I am very sure that they would be good Christians.

Alongside these sober accounts, popular legends of miracles done in his name soon spread among the people. He was said to cure cobra bites with his own spittle, to heal beggars of their sores, to raise the dead. When he mastered Tamil, they said he could speak in tongues. What he did, in fact, was listen to people in their greatest need, and preach the gospel to them with absolute conviction and confidence in the sacraments and rites of the Church. His authority was as absolute as his faith was unshakeable.

This makes Xavier a man of his world, rather than of ours. Just as, in Lisbon, for example, he had never thought of condemning the slave trade, even though he had witnessed its effects on human lives at first hand; just as he had never thought it his duty to question the practice of burning heretics at the post – indeed, he had ministered to them by standing and praying beside them as the wood fires were lit – so too, here in India, he began to pray and work for what he called 'unbelievers', as well as for the baptised. A prayer attributed to Xavier reveals his attitudes:

> Eternal God, Creator of all things, remember that the souls of unbelievers have been created by thee and formed to thy own image and likeness. Behold, O Lord, how to thy dishonour hell is being filled with these very souls. Remember that Jesus Christ, thy Son for their salvation suffered a most cruel death. Do not

permit, O Lord, I beseech thee that thy divine Son be any longer despised by unbelievers, but rather, being appeased by the prayers of thy saints and the Church the most holy spouse of the Son, deign to be mindful of thy mercy and forgetting their idolatry and their unbelief bring them to know him whom thou didst send, Jesus Christ, thy Son, Our Lord who is our health, life and resurrection, through whom we have been redeemed and saved to whom be all glory forever. Amen.

Contemporary mission theology has a problem with Xavier at this point, for he displays none of the sensitivities of our own times. He was not interested in inter-faith dialogue; he had no respect for all that was good and valuable in the religious practices of the 'unbelievers' whom he met; he was sickened by what he took to be their 'idolatry and unbelief'. In the core of his being he was as bigoted as any of his ancestors, the people who threw Jews and Moors out of Spain, stripping their country of a wealth of talent in the name of Christian supremacy. He had no understanding at all of the spiritual heritage of Islam.

What we can relate to, however, is his passionate conviction that these people were bound up into Jesus' mission of salvation. The gospel was not simply intended for western Europeans; everyone was to be saved. He gave his life unstintingly to this cause, working by day, praying by night. In its name he became as homeless and displaced as any present-day international traveller – the business man or woman who has to fly umpteen thousand miles each year, living out of suitcases, crashing through time zones, driven by commercial and financial imperatives that would have baffled Xavier. But he would have recognised the behaviour, the manic pursuit of something unobtainable, yet infinitely desirable. In his case the vision was one of extreme simplicity: he wanted everyone, irrespective of colour or caste or class, to know that Jesus was their 'health, life and resurrection'. His was the generosity of an unquestioning heart.

Does this help us read accounts of his work with some of his own enthusiasm, rather than our modern-day reservations about mass baptisms and the long-term nurture of the life of faith? In fact, once they were Christians, Xavier befriended the people in every way he could. On a trip to Manapar, he wrote back to Francis Mansilhas:

> God our Lord knows the troubles I had on the voyage. I went with twenty boats to relieve the Christians who had fled the Badages to the rocks of Cape Comorin. They were dying of hunger and thirst. The wind was so strong that neither by rowing nor by towing could we reach the Cape. When the wind fell I went back again, and did what was possible to help them. It was the most pitiable thing in the world to see those wretched Christians in such trouble. A lot of them come every day to Manapar. They arrive robbed and needy, and have neither food nor clothing.

To find alms for the poor, he hit upon an imaginative solution. He knew that the Queen of Portugal had a special allowance of golden ducats to pay for slippers and shoes. He wrote to her, proposing that this money should be diverted to help the poor of India. She fell in with his plan and found other money, too, to help with his good causes. In Goa, provision was made for a new Catholic university. On Cape Comorin, Xavier tried to arrange for the safety and well-being of his threatened Christian communities.

Ceylon, Negapatam and San Thome

In December 1544, while on a trip to Cochin to secure this protection, Xavier heard of another and far more extensive massacre of the Christian community in Ceylon. He travelled up to the Gulf of Cambay, presented himself to the Governor of India, and asked how he could help. He learned of the complicated religious history of Colombo, where the Portuguese had first arrived in Ceylon. This was a country riven by religious dissent, where Muslims, Brahmans and Hindus were in constant conflict and embattled Cingalese and Tamils failed to close ranks against the invading Westerners.

Within months, Xavier was in Negapatam, waiting for a passage to Ceylon. Before he left, he wrote to Ignatius begging for help with his labours, for wherever he went he saw the need for more Jesuits to take up the work he had initiated. In the event, he found it difficult to get into Ceylon because of political intrigue. He wrote to Mansilhas, 'I do not know what will become of me. May God our Lord grant us at the right time knowledge of his most holy will, and make us ready to fulfil it whenever it is clearly revealed and made known to us. For to be good we have to be pilgrims in this life, ready to go wherever we can best serve God our Lord.' Xavier's missionary vocation was sorely tested, for he genuinely did not know whether to go back to his pearl fishers or to strike out further east.

He sought God's will by retreating up the eastern coast of India to San Thome. This city was the supposed resting place of St Thomas the Apostle's body, following his death there. Like Goa, it was a smart, colonised city. Xavier found lodgings with a priest and gave himself up to prayer. Here he could rest and recover, and his spirit could mend. He wrote,

> In this holy house I took it as a duty to occupy myself in praying to God to grant me to know in my soul his most holy will, and to give me the firm resolution to fulfil it. It pleased God to remember with his accustomed mercy, and with much interior comfort I felt and knew that it was his will that I should go to those parts of Malacca where Christians have lately been made. If Portuguese ships do not go this year, I will go in some Moorish or heathen ship. I have such faith in God our Lord, dearest brothers, for whose love alone I make this journey, that though no ship at all left the coast this year, and a catamaran was leaving, I would go in it confidently, with all my hope placed in God.

Malacca and the Moluccas

Malacca was the Singapore of the sixteenth century. When Xavier arrived there at the end of September 1545, it was a crossover point for east-

and westbound trade. To his delight, he found letters waiting him. They told him that the Society of Jesus was well established now, and enjoying papal approval as well as an increase in numbers. He wrote back immediately,

> When I got to Malacca a number of letters from Rome and Portugal were given to me, from which I got, and still do get, great comfort. I read them so often that it seems to me that I am there, or that you, dear brothers, are here, and if not in body at least in spirit. Above all, I pray you by the love of God to send out a number of our Company every year, for they are needed, and for going out among the heathen scholarship is not necessary, but that they should come very well drilled in the Exercises.

He was to revise his opinion on the question of scholarship and learning, but never on the importance of a ministry based on giving the Spiritual Exercises. In Malacca he immediately set about translating prayers into the language of the people. He ministered as he had done in Goa, recalling the people to the practice of their faith, encouraging them in their devotional life and offering them the sacraments.

By now Xavier was in charge of the Jesuits' Indies mission as well as being the Papal Nuncio (representative) in the east. In the light of this charge, he decided to press on, going first of all to the Moluccas, islands to the south of the Philippines. He set off on 1 January 1546 and arrived at Amboina in mid-February.

He was now in the Spice Islands, a rich source of trade in cloves and nutmeg, both of which were used for cooking and valued in East and West alike for their medical and cosmetic properties. Once again he found Christians who had been evangelised and abandoned and set about ministering to them, hearing their confessions, marrying them, baptising their children and preaching the word of God to them. He ventured into the interior and reported on strange sights when he got back: a peculiar billy goat, for instance, which could produce kids and provide milk for them.

Worse was to follow than this harmless example,

however, as his brethren in Rome realised when they received his next letter:

The people of these islands are very barbarous and full of treachery. They are baser than the black tribes – an utterly thankless people. There are islands here in which men eat one another. This is those who are killed in battle when there is war, and not otherwise. The hands and heels of those who die naturally are eaten at a great banquet. The people are such barbarians that in some islands a man who wishes to have a great feast will ask his neighbour for the loan of his father, if he is very old, for eating, and promises to give his own father when he is old and the neighbour wants to have a banquet. I hope within a month to go to an island where those killed in war are eaten, and in it also men lend their fathers when they are old for banquets. The inhabitants wish to be Christians, and this is why I am going there. There are abominable fleshly sins among them that you could not believe, nor do I dare to write.

The islands are temperate, with great and

thick woods and plenty of rain. They are so mountainous and difficult to travel that in war the people go up them for defence, so that they are their forts. There are no horses, nor could riding be possible. Land and sea often quake. When the sea quakes those who are sailing think the ship has struck a rock. To see the earthquake is frightful, and still more the sea. Many of the islands cast out fire with a greater noise than any discharge of artillery, however heavy. In the places where the fire comes out, very large stones are carried with it by the great impetus with which it comes. For lack of anyone to preach in these islands the torments of hell, God permits hell to open for the confusion of the infidels and their abominable sins.

Each of these islands has a language of its own, and there is an island where nearly every village has a different language. The Malay language, which is spoken in Malacca, is very general here. When I was in Malacca, I translated with great labour into this language the Creed, with an exposition of the articles, the General Confession, *Paternoster, Ave Maria, Salve Regina,* and the Commandments, so that they may understand when I speak to them of matters of importance. There is one great lack in all these islands: they have no writings, and very few can write. They write in Malay, and the letters are Arabic, which the Moorish *cacizes* (priests) taught, and teach at present. Before they became Moors they could not write.

After this account, his journey to the Islas de Moro could hold few fears, but nevertheless he wrote home with his misgivings:

The land of Moro is very dangerous because its people are very treacherous and put poison in food and drink. So the people who should have looked after the Christians stopped going there. On account of the need of those Christians of Moro for spiritual doctrine, and their need of somebody to baptise them for the salvation of their souls, and also on account of the need I have of losing my temporal life to succour the spiritual life of my neighbour, I determined to go myself to Moro to help the Christians there in spiritual things.

One of the strangest tales about Francis Xavier dates from this time. Here is the account as given by one Fausto Rodriguez.

> Voyaging one day from Amboina to another island, Xavier in his boat was assaulted by furious headwinds. He took from his breast his crucifix, which was about a finger in length, and from the side of the boat dropped it into the sea by its cord. But the cord slipped from his hands and the waves swallowed up the crucifix. He was greatly distressed by the loss and made no secret of his grief. The following day, twenty-four tempestuous hours after the disaster to his crucifix, he reached the Island of Veranula [old Portuguese name for Ceram].
>
> Accompanied by a man named Fausto Rodriguez born at Viana de Alvito [Portugal], he had walked about five hundred paces along the shore towards the village of Tamalo when both he and Rodriguez saw a crab come out of the sea with the crucifix held upright in its claws or pincers. The new standard-bearer of Christ crawled towards the Saint and stood

46

before him with the divine banner hoisted. Xavier went on his knees, and the crab waited until he had taken the crucifix, whereupon it immediately returned to the sea. The Saint kissed his recovered treasure a thousand times and pressed it to his heart. He remained on his knees in prayer for half an hour, as did his companion also, both giving God their profoundest thanks for so illustrious a miracle. That, and nothing more, is known of the sworn testimony taken from Fausto Rodriguez.

The threat of death was ever present, but with the perils of such places as the Islas de Moro behind him, Xavier was now resolved to go to the most extreme and dangerous of places. Nothing could deter him. In the Spice Islands, he had lived surrounded by blue seas and sharp banks of coral, the scent of frangipani, vanilla, coconut palms and tamarind trees blended with cloves, nutmegs and pepper. Now another climate and different vegetation awaited him, as well as a brand new drink – a cup of tea.

Japan

On his return to Malacca, he heard of a new discovery from some Portuguese merchants. 'There, according to the Portuguese, much fruit might be gained for the increase of our holy faith, more than in any other part of the Indies, for they are a people most desirous of knowledge, which the Indian heathen are not.' The judgment is rather brutal by our standards, but Xavier had just met a soul-mate, a Japanese called Yajiro: 'He came to seek me with a great desire to know about our religion. If all the Japanese are like this, so eager to learn as Yajiro, I think they are the most enquiring people in all the lands hitherto discovered.'

So Japan beckoned, and once again Xavier took ship. He returned from Malacca to Cochin in December 1547, confident that 'I or some one of our Company will go to Japan within two years, although it is a very dangerous voyage, both because of great tempests and of Chinese thieves who sail that sea to rob.' From Cochin he wrote begging his brethren in Rome to send missionaries to follow up his work in the Indies. 'I do beg you,' he wrote to Ignatius, 'for the Lord

Jesus' sake, to look on those children of yours in India, and send out some man pre-eminent in virtue and sanctity whose vigour and ardour may arouse my torpor.'

These are the words of a tired man. To the King of Portugal, he gave the reason for his torpor: 'I, Sire, am not quite determined to go to Japan, but I am thinking that I will, for I quite despair of any real chance in India for the increase of our holy faith.' To another Jesuit, Simon Rodriguez, he was even more explicit. He reproached the King for not backing up his mission to the Indies with what he called 'spiritual fundamentals'. In real terms, that meant both personnel and money. For Xavier could not take the gospel to new lands without the certainty of knowing that his Indian Christians would be adequately cared for, however dismissive he was about them now that he had begun to experience the lure of Japan and Japanese culture.

On 15 August 1549, Xavier duly arrived in Kagoshima. The three-thousand sea-mile voyage was over. Japanese adventure had begun. He thanked God for his Japanese companion, who had received the Christian name Paul. With him he met a brand-new culture, and a very orderly one at that. Whereas he had been able to plunge straight in and take care of the sick or revive flagging Christians in his previous travels, Japan was a totally alien experience. It was also a trial. Everything from the climate to the music to the food was a torture to him. He wrote home to describe his feelings:

> The worst hardships you have hitherto endured are trifling compared with what awaits you when you come to Japan … Believe me, the metal of those who come out here will be well tested … I do not say this as though to give you the impression that the service of God is hard. Indeed no; it is light and easy on condition that a man seeks God by the conquest of his own inclinations. But if he is not resolute in the time of trial, he will never know the infinite bounty of God nor have peace in this weary life, which to live without the intimate realisation of God is not life at all but protracted death …

To the brethren in Goa he sent firm instructions about the clothes and shoes which should be provided for any future Jesuit missionaries. His own were totally inadequate: 'The Fathers coming to Japan must be well provided with clothes made of Portuguese wool. And they must come well shod, for here we are dying of cold.' Not only that, but they were bent double, unaccustomed as they were to sitting on the floor, or to eating from porcelain plates with chopsticks on low tables. So what was so special about a cup of tea? Could it offer any comfort? Valignano, the Jesuit who came to Japan forty years later, wrote home to describe the tea ceremony:

> It is a universal custom in Japan to drink a beverage made with hot water and the crushed berries of a little bush which they call *chaa*. This is held for a great thing among them, so much so that all gentlemen have a special room set aside in their houses for the purpose of drinking the beverage. As hot water in Japanese is *yu* and the name of the bush *chaa*, they call the salon *cha-no-yu*, and it is the most esteemed and venerated thing in Japan ...

None of Xavier's descriptions from India carry the same sense of alienation as those he wrote from Japan. In this country he felt more of an explorer than an evangelist, although he immediately set about translating the text of the Creed and some prayers into the language. His friend Paul helped by securing hospitality for him and setting up meetings with various august monks from Buddhist monasteries. Xavier sat with them, exploring their faith and expounding his own, engaging in a fruitless dialogue as it became more and more apparent that they had few points of genuine encounter.

When he first arrived, he observed, 'In my opinion no people superior to the Japanese will be found among unbelievers. They are of good behaviour, and good generally, and not malicious, marvellously honourable.' In the name of this honour, Xavier was made welcome wherever he went. Yet the converts were few – 'This year about six hundred have become Christians. Many more gave up, not because they did not understand that our faith was true, but because they were afraid of the Duke [the *daimio*, or local leader].' A disastrous visit to Sakay and Kyoto made Xavier take stock, for he met with no success in his missionary endeavours.

He began to realise that he would have to be more politically astute if his attempts were to succeed. In India the rulers had converted or had tolerated Christians for a variety of reasons, not least because the Portuguese offered trading possibilities by way of exchange. In Japan, Xavier would have to pull rank. He abandoned his ragged cotton cassock and put on a Japanese gown before going to Yamaguchi to meet the local *daimio*. He carried the letters which he had concealed up till then: letters from the Bishop of Goa and, more importantly, the King of Portugal, offering friendship to Japan and asking for protection for the missionaries. He also carried with him a handsome striking clock, some spectacles, a musical instrument with a range of seventy notes, some mirrors and European books. The *daimio* was gracious, received them in ways that befitted the rank they had adopted, and gave them the use of an empty monastery. Within two months, more than five hundred people were baptised. The Japanese mission had begun in earnest.

No sooner was it under way than Xavier was off again. This time he was intent on travelling to China and opening up this most remote of empires to the good news of the gospel. He left Japan in November 1551 with five Japanese, some of whom were to undertake studies in Goa, some of whom were delegates to the Portuguese authorities there. The Christian community he left behind would be well tended by the Jesuit brothers who succeeded him, would survive the most terrible persecution in the seventeenth century and then be driven underground. Significantly, the persecution was by fire, for they were burnt to death at the stake. Four centuries later, fire again visited the Catholic community of Nagasaki when their cathedral was at the epicentre of the nuclear explosion during World War II. There were Catholics who interpreted this experience in theological terms, and who saw their destiny as a redemptive one. To their mind the Christian community was called to suffer persecution in this way, and thereby to share in the atoning work of Jesus.

China

The route to China lay by way of Cochin. Xavier arrived there on 24 January 1552, unaware that this was to be the last year of his life. He presented himself to the Governor General and described the strategy he had devised for getting into the closed world of the Great Empire. An ambassador should be appointed to visit the King of China on behalf of the King of Portugal. He had just the man in mind, one Diego Pereira, a merchant with whom he had travelled part of the way back from Japan, a rich man who was prepared to put thirty thousand ducats into the project. The Governor agreed to the scheme and offered to subsidise it yet further, realising that if it were to succeed, the ambassadorial visit would have to be lavish in the extreme.

Xavier withdrew to Goa to prepare himself, whilst Pereira went on to Malacca to prepare the booty. When Xavier joined him there at the end of May, trouble flared from an unexpected quarter. Another Portuguese merchant, a man called Alvaro d'Ataide, who had crossed swords earlier with Xavier, now maintained that he should have been the ambassador. As Captain-General of the Sea, he wielded influence and won the day. Pereira was forced to stay in Malacca while Xavier sailed for Singapore. By August he had reached Sancian, to the west of Hong Kong, which served as a rendezvous point for foreign travellers.

Protracted attempts to enter China went on and on as Xavier attempted now one ploy, now another to get in. His little company dwindled yet further when one of them fell ill. Eventually only Antonio, his Chinese aide, was left. On 13 November he wrote what was to be his final letter:

Since this voyage to go from this port to China is difficult and dangerous, I do not know what will fall out, yet I hope that it will fall out well. If by chance I do not enter Canton this year, I will go, as I have already said, to Siam. And if I do not go from Siam to China within the year, I will go to India. Yet I have much hope of getting to China … If God will, I shall not die, though it is a long time since I felt so little inclined to live as I do now …

A junk was promised for 19 November to take him to China. The day came and went; Xavier's spirits fell. That night he rowed out to the *Santa Croce,* the ship which had transported them from Malacca. All the other ships from the fleet had left the harbour. He spent the night on board and then returned to Sancian, carrying a pair of boots and a few almonds given to him by a sailor.

Xavier became ill with a fever and fell into a decline. On 3 December 1552, he died. A faithful witness to his last illness, Antonio, the Chinese man who had accompanied him to the very end, later wrote:

So he remained until the eighth day of his illness. On that day he lost the power of speech altogether and continued silent for three days, until midday on Thursday. During that time he recognised nobody and ate nothing. At noon on Thursday he regained his senses, but spoke only to call upon the Blessed Trinity, Father, Son and Holy Ghost, always one of his tenderest devotions. I heard him again repeat the words: *Jesus, Son of David, have mercy on me,* and he exclaimed again and again: O *Virgin Mother of God, remember me!* He continued to have these and similar words on his lips until the night of Friday passed on towards the dawn of Saturday, when I could see that he was dying and put a lighted candle in his hand. Then, with the name of Jesus on his lips he rendered his soul to his Creator and Lord with great repose and quietude.

In the end, China eluded Francis Xavier. In death – as in life – the apostle of the Indies was recalled to the certainty that 'to be good we have to be pilgrims', for heaven is our home. He was canonised by Pope Gregory XV on 12 March 1622.

PART THREE

Readings

When Francis Xavier wrote home from his mission among the pearl fishers, he described how he brought people to belief in God and nourished their faith:

On Sundays I gather together all the folk, men and women, old and young, to say the prayers in their language; they seem very happy, and come with great joy. We begin with the Confession of One God, Three in One, with loud voices repeating the Creed in Malabar, I saying it first, and then they all repeating it. When the Creed is said, I by myself go over it again article by article, treating each of the twelve separately. I make them see that to be a Christian is nothing if it is not to believe firmly and without hesitation the Twelve Articles: then, when they confess themselves Christians, I ask them concerning each of the Articles if they firmly believe it ... I make them repeat the Creed oftener than the other formulas, because only if he believes the Twelve Articles can a man call himself a Christian.

The only book he ever wrote was his exposition of the Creed. It is reproduced here in full, as it enables the contemporary reader to see how central the dynamics and even the text of the Spiritual Exercises were to his thinking and to his teaching.

Exposition of the Apostles' Creed

1. Christians, rejoice to hear and know how God in creation made everything for the use of men. First He created heaven and earth, angels, sun, moon and stars, birds and beasts that live in the land and the rivers, and the fish that live in the waters; and when all things had been created at last He created man in His likeness.

2. The first man whom God created was Adam, the first woman Eve; and after God created Adam and Eve in the terrestrial Paradise, He blessed and married them, and commanded them to have children and to people the land; and from Adam and Eve we, all the peoples of the world, come; and since God did not give Adam more than one wife, clearly it is in opposition to God that Moors and heathen and bad Christians have many wives.

3. And also it is true that fornicators live in opposition to God, since God first married Adam and Eve before He commanded them to increase and multiply having legitimate children [sons of blessing]. And thus those who adore idols as the unbelievers do, and those who believe in witch-craft, in lots and in diviners, sin greatly against God, for they adore and believe in the devil and take him for their lord, forsaking the God who created them, and gave them soul and life and body and all they have. These miserable creatures by their idolatries lose heaven, which is the place of souls, and the glory of Paradise, for which they were created.

4. But the true Christians and loyal to their God and Lord believe and adore willingly and

heartily the one God and Lord, true creator of heaven and of earth. And well they show it when they go to the churches and see the images which are the reminders of the Saints who are with God in the Glory of Paradise.

5. So Christians put their knees on the ground when they are in the churches, and lift their hands to the heavens where is the Lord God, who is all their good and comfort, and confess in the words of St Peter, '*I believe in God, Father Almighty, Creator of Heaven and earth.*' God created the angels in the heavens before the men in the earth. St Michael, chief of all, and the greater part of the angels at once adored the Lord God, giving Him thanks and praises that He had created them: Lucifer, on the contrary, and many angels with him, were not willing to adore their Creator, but said with pride, Let us go up and be like God who is in the high heavens, and for the sin of pride God thrust Lucifer and the angels with him from Heaven to hell.

6. Lucifer, in envy of Adam and Eve, the first

human beings who were there created in grace, tempted them with the sin of pride in the terrestrial Paradise, telling them they would be as gods if they ate of the fruit which their Creator had forbidden them. Adam and Eve, desirous of being as gods, consented to the temptation of the enemy, and conquered by the demon they forthwith ate of the forbidden fruit, and so lost the grace in which they were created, and for their sins the Lord God thrust them out of the terrestrial Paradise. Outside it they lived nine hundred years in trouble, doing penance for the sin they had committed; and so great was their sin that neither Adam nor his sons could satisfy it, nor again gain the glory of Paradise which they had lost by their pride of wishing to be as God, so the gates of Heaven were shut upon Adam and his sons because of their sin.

7. Oh, Christians, what will become of us the wretched? If the demons for a sin of pride were thrust from the heavens to hell, and Adam and Eve for another sin of pride from the terrestrial Paradise, how shall we, miserable sinners,

ascend to the heavens with such sins, and we so clearly lost?

8. The High God, sovereign and powerful, moved with pity and compassion, seeing our great misery, sent the angel St Gabriel from the heavens to the city of Nazareth, where was the Virgin Mary, with a message which said: 'God hail thee, Mary, full of grace, the Lord be with thee: blessed art thou among women: the Holy Spirit will come over thee, and the virtue of the highest God will lighten thee, and what will be born of thee will be called Jesus, Son of God.' The Virgin St Mary answered the angel St Gabriel: 'Behold the servant of the Lord; be His will done in me.' In the same instant that the Virgin St Mary obeyed the message which St Gabriel brought her from God, the Holy Spirit formed in the womb of this Virgin a human body of her virgin blood; together He created a soul in the same body, and the second Person of the Most Holy Trinity, God the Son, in that instant was incarnate in the womb of the Virgin Mary, thus uniting and joining that soul and the so

holy body; and from the day that the Son of God was incarnate until the day of His birth nine months passed.

9. At the end of this time Jesus Christ, Saviour of all the world, being God and true man, was born of the Virgin Mary, remaining virgin in the birth and after as before it: And St Andrew confessed it, saying, *I believe in Jesus Christ, Son of God, our only Lord;* and after him at once St John said, *I believe that Jesus Christ was conceived of the Holy Spirit and born of the Virgin Mary.* In Bethlehem, near to Jerusalem, Christ our Redeemer was born: then the angels and the Virgin His mother, with her spouse Joseph, and the three ['Kings' inserted in one manuscript] and many others, adored Him as Lord.

10. But Herod, who was evil, being king in Jerusalem, with the covetousness of reigning, desired to kill Him. Joseph was advised by an angel to flee from Bethlehem to Egypt, and he took Jesus Christ and the Virgin His mother, because Herod desired to kill Jesus. St Joseph went to Egypt with Christ and His mother, where he was until Herod died of an evil death; for he was so cruel that in Bethlehem and its neighbouring villages he killed all the men children from two years downwards, thinking that he would kill Jesus Christ among them. After Herod died, the Virgin and St Joseph with the Child Jesus returned to their own country, to the city of Nazareth, by command of the angel.

11. When Christ was twelve years He went up from Nazareth to the Temple of Jerusalem, where were the doctors of the law, and He expounded to them the Scriptures of the Prophets and Patriarchs, who spoke of the coming of the Son of God, and all were astonished when they saw His wisdom. Returning to Nazareth, He was there until the age of nearly thirty years; and then He went to the river Jordan, where St John Baptist was baptising many people: and in this river Jordan St John baptised Jesus Christ; and from there Christ went to the wilderness, where for forty days and forty nights He did not eat. The demon in the wilderness, without knowing

that Jesus Christ was Son of God, tempted Him with three sins – that is to say, gluttony, covetousness, and vainglory.

12. And in all the temptations Christ conquered the demon. And from the wilderness with victory He descended to Galilee and converted many people, and commanded the demons to come out of the bodies of the people, and the demons obeyed the command of Jesus Christ, coming out of the bodies of the men where they were; and the people who saw this were astonished and said: 'Who is this, whom the demons obey?' So the fame of Jesus Christ grew greatly among the people, because they saw that the demons obeyed Him, and that He did many miracles. The men who heard the holy preaching of Jesus Christ and saw the great power which He had over the demons began to believe in Jesus Christ, and brought Him the sick: He cured all of whatsoever infirmity they had.

13. And afterwards Christ called the twelve Apostles and the seventy-two Disciples, and took them in His company around the districts where He was teaching the mysteries of the Kingdom of God. Christ preached to the people, and did miracles which proved the truth of what He preached. In the presence of the Apostles and Disciples Christ gave sight to the blind, speech to the dumb, hearing to the deaf, and life to the dead: He healed the lame and the maimed. The Apostles and Disciples who saw this each time believed more and more in Jesus Christ. Christ gave them such wisdom and virtue that they preached to the people, though they were fishers who had no learning except what the Son of God taught them. In the name and virtue of Jesus Christ the Apostles did miracles, healing many infirmities, casting the demons from the bodies of men in sign that what they preached of the coming of the Son of God was the truth.

14. Such was the fame of Jesus Christ and His Disciples among the people that the principal Jews agreed to kill Him, in their envy of Him and His works, for they saw that all followed and praised the teaching of Jesus.

15. When the Pharisees recognised that they were losing the honour and credit which they formerly had among the Jews before Jesus Christ was manifested to the world, moved with envy, they took Jesus Christ, insulted Him freely, carrying Him from one house to another, scorning and making a mock of Him.

16. And because of the great hate the Pharisees had of Jesus Christ they carried Him to the house of Pontius Pilate, where the Pharisees accused Him with false witnesses, and Pilate, to please the Jews, scourged Jesus Christ so cruelly that from the feet to the head all His holy body was wounded; and, thus cruelly scourged, Pilate handed Him to the Jews to crucify Him.

17. And before they crucified Him they put on the head of Jesus Christ a cruel crown of thorns, and a reed in His right hand; and the soldiers, to make a mock of Jesus Christ, placed themselves on their knees before Him, saying, 'God hail You, King of the Jews,' and spitting in His face and buffeting Him; and with a reed He carried they struck Him on the head, and, finally, on Mount Calvary, near Jerusalem, the Jews crucified Jesus Christ, and thus Christ died on the Cross to save sinners; so that the most holy Soul of Jesus Christ was truly separated from His most precious and most holy body when He expired on the Cross, the divinity being always united with the most holy soul of our Redeemer Jesus Christ, the same divinity remaining with the most holy and precious body of Christ on the Cross and in the sepulchre.

18. And at the death of Jesus Christ the sun was darkened, ceasing to give its light; the whole earth trembled, and the rocks divided, striking one another; the monuments of the dead opened, and many of the holy men rose and went to the city of Jerusalem, where they appeared to many; and those who saw these signs in the death of Jesus Christ said, 'Truly Jesus Christ was the Son of God'; and because this is so the Apostle James said: *I believe that Jesus Christ suffered under the power of Pontius Pilate, was crucified, and dead and buried.* Jesus Christ was God, since He was the second person of the most Holy Trinity, and also He was true man, since He was son of the Virgin Mary and had a rational soul and human body; and inasmuch as He was man, truly He died on the Cross when He was crucified; for death is nothing else but a separation of the soul, leaving the body to which it gave life, and the most holy soul of Jesus Christ was separated from the body when He expired on the Cross.

19. Then, having expired, the most holy soul of Jesus Christ, being united to the divinity of God the Son, as it had always been from the instant when the Lord God created it, descended to Limbo, which is a place below the ground, where were the Holy Fathers, Prophets, and Patriarchs and many other just men, waiting for the Son of God, Jesus Christ, who was to withdraw them from Limbo and take them to Paradise.

20. In every time, beginning with Adam and Eve until now, were men good and bad; the good, being friends of God, reproved with words of truth the evil for their vices and sins, because they offended God, their Lord and Creator; and the bad, being slaves and captives of the demon, persecuted the good, friends of God, taking them, and exiling them, and wounding them, and killing them, and doing them many evils: so that when the *good* died their souls went to Limbo; and the Limbo because it is below the ground is called inferno [hell].

21. Lower than Limbo is a place called Purgatory: to this Purgatory go the souls of those who, when they die, are without mortal sin, and on account of the past sins, which they did in their life, and for which before their death they had not made complete penance, go to Purgatory, where are very great torments of fire, in order to pay the evils and sins done in their life; and when they have paid the penance of their sins, they issue from Purgatory, and go at once to Paradise.

22. The last place which is below the ground is called the infernal hell *[inferno infernal],* where are great torments of fire and miseries: if men would

think on this for an hour daily, and if they knew the troubles of the infernal hell, they would not sin as they do: in this hell is Lucifer, and all the demons who were thrust out of heaven, and all who die in mortal sin. Those who go to this hell have no remedy of salvation, but for ever and ever and without end of ends have to be in it.

23. Oh, brothers! how is it that we have so little fear of going to hell, since every day we do the greatest sins ? It is a sign that we have little faith, since we live like men who do not believe in the *inferno infernal*. The Church and the Saints who are with God in Heaven never pray for those in hell, for these have no remedy to go to Paradise; but the Church and the Saints pray for the dead who are in Purgatory and for the living.

24. Jesus Christ died on Friday, and the most holy soul of Jesus Christ, always united with the divinity, descended to Limbo, and drew all the souls which were then in Limbo waiting for Him. Then on the third day, which is the Lord's Day, He rose from among the dead, His most holy soul again taking the same body which it left when He died on the Cross. After that Jesus Christ rose again in a glorious body, he appeared to the Virgin Mary, His Mother, and to the Apostles and Disciples, and to His friends, who were sad for His death; and with His Glorious Resurrection He consoled the sad and disconsolate, pardoning sinners their sins; and many believed in Jesus Christ, after they saw Him rise again from among the dead, who formerly were not willing to believe that He should die and rise again. And St Thomas affirmed that this is true when he said: *I believe that Jesus Christ descended to the hells, and on the third day rose again from the dead.*

25. And after Jesus Christ rose again He was forty days in this world, teaching the Disciples what they had to believe and do and teach the world in order to go to Paradise; and in this time He showed His Holy Resurrection to be true, and those who doubted in His death, that He would not rise again: and in those forty days He appeared to the Apostles and Disciples, and to many other of His friends, who doubted that He would not rise again when they saw Him die on Mount Calvary on the Cross. And in these forty days those who did not believe during the Passion and Death of Jesus Christ that He was to rise again on the third day completely believed without ever doubting that He was the true Son of God, Saviour of the whole world, since He rose to life from death.

26. At the end of the forty days Jesus Christ went to the Mount Olivet, whence He was to ascend to the high heavens, and with Him went the Virgin Mary, His Mother, and His Apostles and Disciples, and many others; and from this Mount Olivet Jesus ascended to the high heavens in body and in soul, and carried in His company to the glory of Paradise all the souls of the Holy Fathers whom He drew from Limbo. The gates of the heavens opened when Jesus Christ ascended to the high heavens, the angels of Paradise came to accompany Jesus Christ to carry Him with great glory to God the Father, whence to save sinners He descended in the womb of the glorious Virgin Mary, taking human flesh to pay in it our debts; so that Jesus Christ, Son of God, for sins became man, was born, died, rose again, ascended to the heavens, where He is seated at the right hand of God the Father. And since this is truth, James the Less said: *I believe that Jesus Christ ascended to the heavens, and is seated at the right hand of God the Father Almighty.*

27. And since this world had a beginning, it is bound to have an end, and so it will finish, and thus as Jesus ascended to the heavens so He will descend to give each one what he deserved; and so it is true that all who believe in Jesus Christ and keep His commandments will be judged that they may go to the glory of Paradise; and those who would not believe in Jesus Christ, such as the Moors, Jews, and heathen, will go to hell without any redemption. Bad Christians who would not keep the ten commandments will be judged by Jesus Christ to go to hell.

28. At the end of the world all then living will die, for every man is born with this condition that he must die: since Jesus Christ our Redeemer died and rose again for sins, we all must die and rise again. Besides this, the bodies of good men who may be alive at the end of the world will not be holy and glorious, or ready to ascend with them to heaven; therefore they must die; and in their resurrection they will take the same bodies, yet not subject to suffering as formerly. So when Jesus Christ descends from heaven on the day of judgement to judge the good and the bad, all will rise again, beginning from the first to the last who died. And as this is truth, St Philip said: *I believe that Jesus Christ will come from Heaven to judge the living and the dead.*

29. When we Christians bless ourselves we confess the truth as to the most Holy Trinity, that there are three persons, one God. The first is the person of God the Father, and the second person of God the Son, and the third person of God the Holy Spirit; and all three persons are one only God, threefold and one. God the Father is not made nor created nor begotten. The Son of God the Father is begotten and not made nor created. The Holy Spirit proceeds from the Father and from the Son, not created, nor made, nor begotten. When we make the sign of the Cross we show this order of proceeding, placing the right hand on the head, saying *in the Name of the Father,* in sign that God the Father is not made nor created nor begotten; and then placing the hand on the breast, saying *and of the Son,* in sign that the Son was begotten of the Father, and not made nor created; and then placing the hand on the left shoulder, saying *and of the Holy;* and passing the right hand by the head to the right shoulder, saying *Spirit,* in sign that the Holy Spirit proceeds from the Son and from the Father.

30. Every good Christian is obliged to believe firmly, without doubting, in the Holy Spirit and in His holy inspirations, which protect us from doing evil, and move our hearts to keep the ten commandments of God, and the commandments of the holy universal Mother Church, and to fulfil the works of mercy, corporal and spiritual. And as this is truth, the Apostle St Bartholomew said: *I believe in the Holy Spirit.*

31. All we faithful Christians are obliged to believe, without doubting, what the Apostles and Disciples and Martyrs and all the Saints of Jesus Christ believed of Jesus Christ concerning all that is necessary to believe for our salvation, as to His divinity and humanity, for Jesus Christ was God and true man. Also in general we are obliged to believe firmly, without doubting, in all that those who rule and govern the universal Church of Jesus Christ believe, for they are inspired and ruled by the Holy Spirit in what they have to do as to the government of the universal Church in the matters of our holy faith, in the which they cannot err, because they are ruled by the Holy Spirit. We must also believe the Scriptures of our religion, and of Jesus Christ; and further we are obliged to believe such of the holy canons and councils as are ordered by the Church, and the ordinances made by the Pope, Cardinals, Patriarchs, Archbishops, and Bishops, and Prelates of the Church, when in all these things, without doubting, we believe all that those who rule and govern the universal Church of Jesus Christ believe. This is what the Apostle

Evangelist St Matthew charged when he said: *I believe in the holy Catholic Church.*

32. And so we true Christians believe that the good works and merits of Jesus Christ are communicated to and profit all other Christians who are in a state of grace: and as in the natural body the works of one member profit all the body, so it is in the spiritual body (which is the Church).

33. And as chiefly from the head there descends to the members and is communicated to them their sustentation, so from Christ our Lord, only begotten Son of God, who is Head of all the true faithful, there is communicated spiritual sustentation by means of the seven sacraments of the Church — that is to say, by baptism, by confirmation (which we call chrism), by the Most Holy Sacrament of the altar, by the sacrament of penance, by the extreme unction, by the sacrament of the orders, by matrimony. For whoever takes duly any one of these sacraments is granted grace by which his soul lives spiritual life, which Christ our Lord, only begotten Son of God, merited by

the most holy works He did in this world, labour-
ing and suffering injuries and the death of the
Cross to free sinners from the captivity of the
demon and to turn them to the true knowledge of
their God, communicating to them His own merits. And not only are the merits of the Son of God
communicated, as from the head to the other
members, but further those of the other saints are
communicated to all the faithful, who are in grace,
as the goods of one member of the body are communicated to the other members of the same body.

34. Christians further confess and believe: that
God our Lord has power to pardon the sins by
which the sinners separate themselves from Him,
and lose the grace which He had before communicated to them: and that this power He gives
and communicates to the priests of the Catholic
Church, by which communication they now
have power to absolve from sins those whom
they find worthy to be absolved before God.

35. And accordingly men must so prepare to do
what they are obliged for the safety of their soul,

so that the priests may judge them (in conformity to what God commands) as worthy to be absolved; and having done this and having confessed at the obligatory times, and being absolved by the priest, they again gain the grace of God, and are pardoned their sins. And this is what St Matthias said: *I believe in the communion of Saints and the remission of sins.*

36. And because it is a just thing to believe in the goodness of our Lord and His infinite mercy which will not leave without reward those who serve Him in this life, nor without chastisement those who offend and break His precepts: we believe in the resurrection of the flesh, which is to say, that we all have to rise again in the body, the very same as we are now, after we have passed temporal death, and that it is certain that our Lord, according to His justice, will then give for ever the reward to the bodies which in this world for His love suffered troubles and persecutions, and were afflicted for not consenting in sins; and since their souls shared in trouble, they also may enjoy glory and rest.

37. And on the contrary (we believe) that the bodies of the bad, who in this life cared to do their own will and fulfil their appetites rather than keep the law of God our Lord, should be eternally chastised in the hells, since they offended the eternal Lord God, their resurrection will be made in the day of final judgement, when all born in this life must rise in body and soul: the bad to be cast into hell for their sins, and the good to enter the glory of Paradise with God our Lord. And this is what St Thaddeus said: *I believe in the resurrection of the flesh.*

38. And as our soul is like God almighty and eternal in so far as it is spiritual, and in the powers which God Himself gave it – that is to say, will, understanding and memory – and the desire of men is to last for ever, it is meet that a creature, so excellent as is man, should fulfil this longing, and so all we Christians believe that it will be fulfilled; and therefore we believe in the life eternal, which we confess will never have end; rather after the resurrection of the flesh, wherein the soul, which never dies, has again to take its body, will live together with it, as they are now united, and by a much better mode, eternally with God, and will enjoy in the heavens, together with the angels, the Presence of their Creator and Lord, and of all the celestial benefits the which are so great that, however much one may in this life think of them and imagine them, it is not possible to reach or understand their grandeur.

39. There the Saints rest, without any opposition; there nothing is lacking of all they can desire; there no evil is found, nor can it be found nor exist, nor is there lacking, nor will ever be lacking, all good, which the blessed will enjoy eternally. And this is what St Matthias said: *I believe in the life eternal.*

FURTHER READING

Brodrick, James, S.J., *Saint Francis Xavier*, Burns
& Oates, 1952

Coleridge, Henry James, S.J., *The Life and Letters of
St Francis Xavier*, 2 vols., Burns & Oates, 1886

Costelloe, M. Joseph, S.J. (trans.), *The Letters and
Instructions of Francis Xavier*, Gujarat Sahity
A. Prakash, 1993

Loyola, Saint Ignatius, *Personal Writings*, translated with notes by Joseph A. Munitiz and
Philip Endean, Penguin, 1996

Stewart, Edith Anne, *The Life of St Francis Xavier:
Evangelist, Explorer, Mystic*, Headley Bros.
Publishers Ltd, 1917

Stranks, C.J., *The Apostle of the Indies*, SPCK, 1933